PRAISE FOR *CHANGE STARTS WITHIN YOU*

"*Change Starts Within You* is the perfect segue to Cortney's electrifying TEDx Talk. If you want to follow the road to success without detouring through burnout and self-disillusionment, McDermott's book will be your trail guide!"

—Nadine Hack, Top 100 Thought Leader on Trustworthy Business Behavior and adviser to Nelson Mandela and President Obama

"Soulful, sassy, and full of practical insights. If *Eat, Pray, Love* married *The 4-Hour Workweek*, McDermott's book would be their firstborn child."

—Monika Lutz, vice president of sales at Voiceplace, author, speechwriter, and Harvard University valedictorian

"Sincere. Entertaining. Actionable."

—Suzanne Pflaum, design strategist at Context Partners

"If you're looking to unearth your vision, *Change Starts Within You* is the key to feeling more free and confident so that you are able to sustain yourself."

—Stacey Roen, traceability manager at Lululemon Athletica

"The world doesn't need another self-help book, but we do need Cortney McDermott's book, *Change Starts Within You*. It's self-awareness without being preachy. Cortney offers insightful wisdom for lasting change through simple strategies to remember that your most precious resource is yourself."

—Betsy Blankenbaker, founding partner of Beautiful Infinity Books and bestselling author of *Autobiography of an Orgasm*

"*Change Starts Within You* was what I needed back when I was searching for the right path for me and learning to trust my intuition. I love this book, and McDermott's simple steps to learning to trust your intuition are priceless."

—Carla Coulson, author of *Italian Joy*, *Paris Tango*, and *Chasing a Dream*

"If you're ready to stop fighting yourself so that you can flow, then you're ready for *Change Starts Within You*. This book guides you on your journey to becoming your truest self. Again."

—Adam James, award-winning singer, songwriter, life coach

"I was thoroughly delighted by the profound wisdom displayed in such a pure and simple format. Thanks to Cortney's tools and powerful exercises, I can now see and feel my Timbuktu."

—Francis Piché, founder of the Resilience Element

Change Starts Within You provides an easy-to-follow road map to help navigate the question that so many of us are facing today: how to make an impact in the world, create abundance, show up for your family and community—*and* maintain a healthy relationship with self and planet. Cortney shows you how to live a sustainable life where anything and everything is possible."

—Élan McAllister, Tony Award–winning Broadway producer and Qoya teacher

"Optimistic, enthusiastic, and encouraging, the words and exercises in this book will help you blaze your own path toward a life that is truly sustainable."

—Kate Snowise, psychologist and life and executive coach at Thrive.How

Change starts within YOU

Change starts within YOU

UNLOCK THE CONFIDENCE TO LEAD WITH INTUITION

—Cortney McDermott

Published by Sustainability Simplicated, Chicago
www.cortneymcdermott.com

Edited and Designed by Girl Friday Productions
www.girlfridayproductions.com
Editorial: Nicole Burns-Ascue
Cover and Interior Design: Rachel Christenson
Author Photo: Alberto Bogo

ISBN (Paperback): 978-0-9989552-0-9
e-ISBN: 978-0-9989552-1-6

Library of Congress Control Number: 2017907272

First Edition

Contents

CHASING

Gold

Stars

SOMETIMES ROCK
BOTTOM CAN LOOK
A LOT LIKE BEING
AT THE TOP TO
EVERYONE ELSE.

Flash back six years: I'm sitting on a private jet, sipping an espresso, newspapers from all over the world neatly stacked beside me, on my way to Brussels for work, and . . . an essential piece of my life is broken.

It's my BlackBerry.

It's locked, courtesy of my two-year-old daughter, and I want to chuck it out the window, I'm so overwhelmed. My mind's racing ahead to all the unanswered e-mails, all the missed calls, the headache of figuring out how to get it fixed while traveling and racing from one meeting to the next.

And that's when a quiet calm sets in and I hear, *Whose dream is this, anyway?*

By society's definitions of success I had it all: a rising career at a Fortune 500 company, publications, awards, husband, daughter, marathon medals, Jimmy Choo heels . . .

Yet inside those designer shoes, I felt cramped. And that wasn't the only signal of stress, or *distress*, that my body was sending. My skin was dry. My hair was fried with yet another straightening treatment. My smile was gone. (And you know you can't fake a smile—it's in the crow's-feet.)

And here's what the layer under the surface looked like: frantically packing for yet another trip, freaking when my daughter decided my BlackBerry was a toy, scrambling all the way to the airport in failed attempts to "reconnect" . . .

On that plane, flying toward Brussels, while everything in my body was flying in the opposite direction, what really worried me was realizing that even if I'd had a working BlackBerry I'd still be in this Mayday mode.

How come no one told me that being successful could feel so miserable?

It was becoming increasingly clear: chasing gold star after gold star, coupled with unrealistic ideas about "work-life balance," was *not* sustainable.

Yet it's very likely I could have gone on collecting badges at an ever-increasing pace if it hadn't been for that visceral nudge that day on the plane:

Whose dream is this, anyway?

Was I living for *me*? Was I honoring my values? What *were* my values? If I wasn't living for me, then who—or what—was it all for?

And that's when I realized: we all care about living and working sustainably; we've just been defining that inadequately. We think *sustainability* means consuming less energy and reducing waste. And while these things absolutely do matter, that macro view has made our micro solution invisible.

We are the missing variable in this equation. It's time to stop looking outside for the solution.

I wrote this book to share what I learned after that fateful day on the plane: how to tune back in, confidently lead from your values, and create a truly sustainable vision.

Change starts within YOU

"EVERYONE THINKS OF
CHANGING THE WORLD,
BUT NO ONE THINKS OF
CHANGING HIMSELF."

—LEO TOLSTOY

SIMPLE SUSTAIN ABILITY

My theory of sustainability is simple: *change starts within you*. If you're making yourself a better person, you're making the world a better place.

And what I mean by that is each of us is like a cell that serves the larger body—whether that body is a community, a company, or the natural world we live in. We each have specific advantages and DNA that only we can contribute. But if we lose sight of what that individual contribution is, we start chasing everyone else's standards.

Burnout, constant comparison, and disconnection are the side effects of this approach.

That's why I created my own definition of sustainability:

the ability to sustain yourself.

You are the answer you are seeking. Learning to sustain yourself is the simplest way to make tomorrow better than today.

Because when you grow and evolve, the world does too.

FILLING NOT TO FEEL

Have you ever filled up with work, food, television, social media, [insert your favorite distraction here] to avoid *feeling*? In our desire to quickly alleviate discomfort, it's easy to just placate or numb any internal signals of distress. We do this in so many different ways, most of which are encouraged socially, meaning it's often difficult to detect the self-sabotage at work.

Everywhere we look we're bombarded with the idea that we're never quite enough and that the latest gadget or next promotion can fill that void. You know the broadcast: you need this [system, product, life hack] to be happy, feel better, look good . . .

This constant searching outside weakens our ability to go within for answers. And the more we neglect listening to ourselves, the less sustainable our lives become.

But it doesn't have to be that way.

TUNE INTO YOUR INTUITION

> *"The intuitive mind is a sacred gift and the rational mind is a faithful servant. We have created a society that honors the servant and has forgotten the gift."*
>
> *—Albert Einstein*

As humans, we've developed the curious and very unusual ability to ignore our intuition.

We can choose—and maybe this is essentially what free will is—to deny any and all instinctual nudges (those same nudges that kept us alive back in the Stone Age). And in the name of realism, achievement, or expediency, we often do.

But ignoring those signals inevitably leads to suffering, because tuning it out does nothing but lead us astray. Our intuition is like an internal GPS: it shows us the quickest way to get us where our higher self wants to go.

Shortly after the Private Jet BlackBerry Incident, I dropped my daughter off to day care before leaving for yet another trip, and bawled my eyes out in the parking lot.

No matter how hard I'd tried to silence it, I knew at this point that my job—my life—was *unsustainable*.

My intuition was signaling to me loud and clear.

I knew I needed to slow down. I also knew that my career was important to me, and I still wanted to be a voice for change in the business world. Only I wanted and needed to do this on my terms and with plenty of time-outs for friends, family, and myself.

But on a rational level I was afraid of what that meant. I was afraid of what people would think if I quit my job to set out on my own and feared I might not have what it takes to be an entrepreneur.

THE FALLACY OF REALISM

> *"All progress depends on the unreasonable man."*
>
> *—George Bernard Shaw*

When we do start to listen to our intuition, we have to be prepared to meet with other people's fears, as well as our own ingrained ideas about what's "practical" or "realistic."

Now that I'd finally started to tune in, it seemed almost everyone was telling me to tune back out.

"Be realistic. You have an amazing job."

"Why don't you just ask to travel less rather than throwing away everything you've worked so hard for?"

"That's totally impractical."

"You better have a plan."

"Are you sure?!"

Luckily, I was also fortunate enough to have a handful of people who reinforced my confidence in what was possible. I chose to tune into that support and encouragement instead of ignoring my intuition and taking the "realistic" route.

Because realists don't change the world. Unrealistic people do.

BE READY TO UNLEARN

Following your intuition, which sometimes means being "unrealistic," also requires a readiness to *unlearn*.

Growing up, I wasn't taught about things like neuroscience, positive psychology, or *The Happiness Advantage*. And what I mean by that is I wasn't taught anything about this magnificent operating system we're all walking around with or how to use it to attract what I wanted. I wasn't even really taught to think for myself.

Instead, I was taught how to memorize facts and pledge my allegiance. Basically, I was raised for an assembly line.

How do we start unlearning what doesn't serve us so we can replace it with what does?

The good news is that you only have to forget what you've been taught long enough to remember and act on what you already know.

PS: ONE OF THE THINGS I HAD TO UNLEARN WAS "SIT STILL! DON'T TALK!" NOW I'M CONSTANTLY ON THE MOVE AND SHARING MY STORY WITH ANYONE WHO'LL LISTEN. HOW ABOUT YOU? WHAT COULD YOU START UNLEARNING?

REMEMBERING WHAT YOU KNOW

> *"You will never be able to escape from your heart. So it's better to listen to what it has to say."*
>
> —*Paulo Coelho*

The stories and exercises on the pages that follow are designed for precisely this purpose—to help you re-member (piece back together) *your* values, your vision, your genius. To channel *your* intuition and live a life that's sustainable for *you*—and the planet.

Spiritual teacher Ram Dass once remarked, "I'm not going to say anything that you don't know already. But the perplexing problem is that you don't know you know." Millennia prior, Plato taught that *all learning is remembering.*

The exercises in this book are simple, but that doesn't mean they're easy.

Going within and tuning into your intuition requires an honest assessment of how you're showing up in the world *right now*.

And also where or how you're not.

And that means you have to *remember* who you are.

Begin Where YOU ARE

WHAT ARE YOUR VALUES?

To make changes in my life and go where I needed to go next, I first needed to understand where I *really* was in that moment. What was it exactly about my life that wasn't sustainable?

Before you can follow your intuition, you have to meet yourself again at a core level. If you don't get in touch with what's true deep inside of you, you'll get sidetracked again and again by realism, expectations, and chasing after the next best thing.

It's not easy meeting your core self—some of us haven't seen it in decades. The best way to start is to get back in touch with your values.

Exercise

WHO'S YOUR HERO?

One day I ran across an exercise that changed my life. It's shortened here to take only a few minutes.

Step 1: Close your eyes and picture one of your heroes. This can be a well-known person or one of your friends, family members, colleagues, or acquaintances. What characteristics, ideals, and qualities does this person have that you admire? What makes them your hero?

Step 2: Open your eyes and take a moment to jot down your hero's name and how you see that person—the values he or she possesses, as well as any other insights you had while your eyes were closed.

COMPLETE STEPS 1 AND 2 BEFORE TURNING THE PAGE TO THE FINAL STEP . . .

Step 3: Now cross out that person's name and write your own. That's you. The attributes you assigned to that person represent your most deeply held values.

These values speak to you, meaning they are your own. The most beautiful qualities you see in another person are your most valuable personality traits. *You couldn't see them in another if you didn't possess them yourself.*

You may not believe this at first. I get it. These values may be latent in you. But keep reading, because we're going to pull them out.

PS: FOR THE FULL HERO EXERCISE, CHECK OUT AYSE BIRSEL'S *DESIGN THE LIFE YOU LOVE*.

SAY HELLO TO YOUR VALUES

"We're all heroes if you catch us at the right moment."

—*John Bubber in* Hero

I was blown away by the surprise ending of this exercise. I *finally* had an authentic list of my own values. I was sure of it. Plus, from then on, whenever I wanted to reconnect with what was most important to me, I could just imagine my heroes. (Somehow imagining those we admire is easier than imagining our best self.)

One of my heroes is Oprah Winfrey. I heard once that she always uses a straw when drinking onstage. Reportedly because, as she says, "Love is in the details." That's a value of mine—creating love in the details and paying attention to the small stuff, because it makes a *huge* difference.

So when I did this exercise, I drew a picture of that straw. Here are the other values I identified in Oprah (ahem, myself):

~~Oprah~~ *Cortney*

- Unshakable faith
- Courage in the face of adversity
- Vision
- Drive
- Intelligence
- Honesty
- Integrity

PS: THIS EXERCISE IS ALSO VERY HUMBLING, BECAUSE IT CAN REVEAL HOW FAR REMOVED WE MAY BE FROM OUR CORE VALUES . . .

LIVING YOUR VALUES

Once you've listed your core values, you can use them as guideposts. A simple yes/no barometer will help you see how you're currently living up to the values in your life, and where you might have some work to do.

For instance, take my husband—another one of my heroes. One of the qualities I listed for him was "committed to family." I knew as soon as I wrote it that this was one area where I wasn't showing up as much as I would have liked. As ashamed as I was to admit it, family had definitely taken second place to my work.

Here are the other qualities I listed for my husband:

- Unconditional love
- Calm, steady, serene
- Quiet confidence
- Sure, not seeking, knows

Having such a clear list of what's truly important for me makes it much easier to step up and show up for it.

The other day I sat down to a puzzle of the world with my daughter. It was a big one, and we had the entire afternoon to work on it. We both became increasingly excited and determined as we started connecting the pieces. We weren't just piecing together a puzzle; we were fully present with one another and the moment, with nowhere to be, nothing else to do. It felt *amazing*.

This is what it feels like when you're connected to what's most important to you—those deeper, higher qualities yearning to be expressed through and as you.

HOW ARE YOU SHOWING UP?

After you identify your core values, the next step is taking a baseline assessment of how you're actually showing up for these values in each core area of your life: physical health, social life, romantic love, career, home/environment, finances, and spirituality/faith.

For example, if one of your values is "being energetic," you might ask yourself if you feel enthusiastic and engaged in your career.

When evaluating how I'm showing up in the core pillars of my life, I use this simple rating scale:

- **ROCK STAR STATUS:** I'm killing it in this area and proud of how I'm showing up.

- **BLAH:** I haven't really considered this area of my life all that much. I'm not unhappy about it, just kind of apathetic.

- **EEK!:** I'm struggling. This area could really use some tender lovin' care, and I know I've been ignoring it.

Now it's time to take your own inventory. The exercise on the next page is designed to help you quickly and easily assess your baseline.

Exercise

TAKE YOUR LIFE PICTURES

Take a picture, or find a picture, of you in each core area of your life, then pull these together to make a big visual assessment of how you're doing overall. For example:

- **Physical:** Get naked.
- **Social:** Grab a recent pic of you with your friends.
- **Love:** Take a picture with your partner, or alone if you're not currently in a romantic relationship.
- **Financial:** Open your wallet or take out your latest bank statement and snap a shot.
- **Purpose/Career:** Take a selfie at your desk, or a photo of a recent project.
- **Home/Environment:** Capture a messy closet or your favorite nook in your house.

- **Spirituality/Faith:** Take a snapshot of an inspiring passage from a book or your favorite element in nature that illustrates your relationship to God or the Universe.

   Add a caption to each photo to describe the current status of that area in life. For example, you could describe your current physical state as "Rock star status! I feel fit and healthy," or "Eek! Definitely room to up my game." Then arrange all the photos together so you have a poster of how you're showing up for what's most important.

   Like the previous one, this exercise is energizing and also humbling!

PS: A POLAROID CAMERA IS MY FAVORITE TOOL FOR THIS EXERCISE, BUT DIGITAL WORKS TOO. OR YOU COULD SIMPLY DRAW A SYMBOL THAT REPRESENTS YOUR STATUS.

KEEP IT SIMPLE

"Simplicity is the ultimate sophistication."

—*Leonardo da Vinci*

Taking your pictures might feel awkward at first, but how can you get where you're going next if you don't know where you are? It'd be like trying to navigate toward Chicago without knowing whether you're in Los Angeles or New York. *Yikes.*

The good news is that the simple exercises you did in this chapter will give you really clear starting points and help steer you to where you need to go next.

Know
WHERE
You're
Going

"WHETHER
YOU THINK YOU CAN, OR
YOU THINK YOU CAN'T—
YOU'RE RIGHT."

—HENRY FORD

VISION MEANS TO SEE CLEARLY

Now that you know where you are, what's the next destination on your map?

I call this your Timbuktu.

I've never been to Timbuktu, nor have I ever met anyone who's been . . . yet I have no doubt that Timbuktu exists and that I could find it if I wanted to.

That, by the way, is true vision.

The original meaning of the word *vision* is "to see clearly in the present." It's not some far-off aspiration or goal that you have to strive and struggle toward. It's your current potential, which is unlimited.

So . . . what's your Timbuktu? What do you see for yourself? What does the full expression of you look like? Close your eyes. What can you imagine? This is your Timbuktu. And by imaging it, you're already on your way there.

When identifying your Timbuktu, remember it's not about a specific material outcome. It's about how you want to be and *feel*.

When we lead with a desired feeling, as opposed to a material result, we remain open to the myriad ways that feeling can surface in our life.

WHAT'S YOUR TIMBUKTU?

When I was working as an assistant at The North Face, I saw myself as a part of the management team. I envisioned being up onstage and presenting my ideas at the sales meeting on opening night.

I had no idea how to go from where I was to where I saw myself, but my desire was strong. I had my starting point and knew my next destination.

More importantly, I wasn't attached to what the outcome looked like. Yes, I'd seen myself up on that stage. But it wasn't the stage or spotlight I was after. It was the feeling of *leading* that I really wanted, and I stayed open to any ways to do that as I made my way to my Timbuktu.

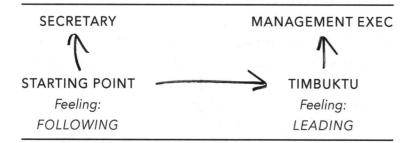

SECRETARY	MANAGEMENT EXEC
↑	↑
STARTING POINT ⟶	TIMBUKTU
Feeling:	*Feeling:*
FOLLOWING	LEADING

The gap between the two became my obsession. (More on that in the next chapter.)

PS: I DID END UP ON THAT STAGE, IF YOU WERE WONDERING. ☺

ONE LAST WORD ABOUT TIMBUKTU

*"If one advances confidently in the
direction of his dreams, and endeavors
to live the life which he has imagined, he
will meet with a success unexpected in
common hours."*

—*Henry David Thoreau*

My faith that Timbuktu is there doesn't require any direct experience.

I love this reminder: Your Timbuktu comes from that very same force that beats your heart and grows your nails, one you never once have to question. You just know it's all taken care of.

Yet think of how many times we sabotage and doubt our vision through the misuse of our rational minds. How often we set out to our very own Timbuktu only to decide halfway through the journey that it's taking too long to get there, or we aren't strong or smart enough to carry on, or maybe it's not there at all, so we might as well turn back or change destinations.

I've had the same vision for years. And part of it included writing the book you're holding now.

I had no idea how that would happen.

Yet setting a vision to live into is part of what heals us, what sustains us, and what inspires others to do the same.

Imagine how sustainable our world could be if every single one of us was living toward his or her Timbuktu.

Exercise

CREATE YOUR LIFE MAP

To map out the way to your Timbuktu, start by grabbing the photo board you made (see pages 35-36) and choose a couple of those EEK! or BLAH pictures.

With those starting points in mind, envision your next destination in those areas. Write down your starting point and your Timbuktu for each.

While making this map, you can keep it simple or use it as an excuse to let your creativity shine. Get out the pens, magazines, markers, stickers, glue. And then start to imagine what you want.

The next stop on your map can be represented by a simple caption or anything else—a magazine clipping, a drawing, or a new picture—that symbolizes what you see for yourself.

Now draw lines or arrows from your starting point toward your Timbuktu in the areas you've chosen. All the white space around those arrows—this is what we call the gap. And while it isn't as defined as your starting point or destination, the gap is actually what it's all about.

When you're done, find a sacred space for your life map. God, the Universe, Spirit—whatever you want to call that power that beats your heart and grows your nails—is calling you to this act of creation. Honor it. And revisit it often.

FROM EEK! TO ROCK STAR

A dear friend of mine is a high-level corporate executive hankering to open a little coffee shop.

Her starting picture could read,

> *"EEK! Strung out, buried in bureaucracy, and missing authentic connection with others."*

Her Timbuktu could read,

> *"I'm inspired and inspiring those around me through my work."*

The space in between can be a series of small steps that move her toward those inspirational feelings.

PS: REMEMBER TIMBUKTU IS YOUR *NEXT*, NOT FINAL, DESTINATION. SO, FOR EXAMPLE, MY FRIEND WOULDN'T HAVE TO COMMIT TO THE FULL-BLOWN COFFEE SHOP. HER VISION COULD SIMPLY BE ABOUT FINDING WAYS TO MORE AUTHENTI-CALLY CONNECT WITH OTHERS (THE *FEELING* SHE'S AFTER).

WHAT I LEAST WANTED TO DO

So now you can see where you're really showing up. And more importantly, where you're definitely *not*.

We all have it: that one thing we do anything to avoid; that thing we're sure we'll never be any good at. For me it was finance. Basically, anything having to do with numbers.

My brain would shut down any time a conversation about money would come up. Or worse, I'd find myself nodding my head, pretending to understand.

But I knew I couldn't go on that way because, well, I have a family to watch out for and I'm also a business owner.

Here's what my financial "picture" would have looked like a few years back.

EEK! How can I figure this out!?

TURNING IT AROUND

One day when I was complaining about my struggles with finances to a mentor and friend, she gave me this advice: "Instead of saying, 'I need to fix my finances,' try saying, 'I am inspired to improve my finances' and see how that feels."

Whoa. That felt *very* different. I reframed and changed the caption on my picture: "I am inspired to learn about finances and apply what I learn." And it suddenly wasn't so scary.

That's when folks such as Ray Dalio, Suze Orman, Robert Kiyosaki, and Anthony Robbins stepped in to demystify money and inspire me even more. Pretty soon I realized I *could* do this.

I started small with tracking my spending. It didn't take all that long to move on to areas that once seemed completely impossible, such as investing and creating a Giving Fund. And while *Fortune* magazine hasn't named me Madame Templeton or anything, I can now hold my own when it comes to money talk.

By changing my approach I was able to take the first step.

> *What's something that's been dragging you down that you can start feeling great about?*

ACT TODAY, NOT TOMORROW

"I do not believe in a fate that will fall on us no matter what we do. I do believe in a fate that will fall on us if we do nothing."

—*Ronald Reagan*

To paraphrase from motivational author Napoleon Hill's work, *knowledge is not power. It's potential power. Knowledge without action is completely useless.*

We could substitute *knowledge* with *vision* here and come to the same powerful conclusion:

You have to act on it.

Taking action is the only way to test those intuitive hunches. It's also the only difference between getting to your Timbuktu or not.

FOCUS
Your Energy
for
Results

CHOOSING WHERE TO START

When you know the next destination(s) on your life map (your Timbuktu), which direction do you head in first? Deciding can be tricky.

The Italians have a saying, *l'imbarazzo della scelta*, or the embarrassment of choice: When we have too many options, it can become difficult to choose. Our brains go into default mode (we do what we've always done) or, worse, crisis mode (we're overwhelmed and paralyzed).

It's too easy to cling to what's familiar—to focus on the areas of life where we've always focused. But doing that won't help us change, and paralysis by analysis won't get us where we're going either.

This time it's different. Relax and listen for the part of your life map that's calling the loudest for your attention. Close your eyes. You know what it is. Focus in on it and commit: this is where you'll start to bridge the gap.

YOU DO HAVE TO CHOOSE

"Faith is taking the first step even when you don't see the whole staircase."

—*Martin Luther King Jr.*

You may look at your map and be tempted to start a bunch of things at once. I understand this feeling.

The Timbuktus on my map include being an energetic, present, playful mother; a supportive, fun wife; and a successful entrepreneur who creates an inspiring and supportive space for my clients and my team to evolve.

So how do I bridge the gap? Well, whether it's coloring with my daughter, grabbing a morning coffee with my husband, or having a dance party with my team, I set aside chunks of time that ensure I'm heading toward my destination.

I can do all of these things. *But just not simultaneously.*

I learned this the hard way early on in my life as an entrepreneur. I wanted to take on everything, all at the same time. And I did. The result: I had way too much on my plate and was unable to meet my standards for any of it. Not a good feeling . . .

FOCUS: FOLLOW *ONE* COURSE UNTIL SUCCESSFUL

In a keynote speech about the "third metric," Arianna Huffington discusses the dangers of multitasking: "You think you're being efficient, but actually you're being stupid."

As Arianna points out, we now have scientific evidence proving we cannot successfully multitask.

What you're really doing when you think you're multitasking is shifting your attention from one thing to another at an astonishing pace. While it's fascinating we have this capability, it's not exactly the best use of our mental faculties.

When, instead, we Follow *One* Course Until Successful, we actually accomplish more, better, and feel less stressed.

PS: TO READ MORE ABOUT ARIANNA HUFFINGTON'S PERSONAL WAKE-UP CALL WITH MULTITASKING, CHECK OUT HER BOOK *THRIVE: THE THIRD METRIC TO REDEFINING SUCCESS AND CREATING A LIFE OF WELL-BEING, WISDOM, AND WONDER.*

PRIORITIZING YOUR PRIORITIES

Bring one destination from your map to the forefront of your life, prioritize it, and nurture it little by little. Once it's thriving, you can bring in another Timbuktu, until you are actively working toward all the ways you want to show up in life.

For example, today—or as soon as you can—decide what you'll prioritize and then eliminate all distractions for the time you spend on this priority. Select something small to start out.

Next, put a "focus session" note on your door, turn off the Wi-Fi, unplug the Ethernet, silence cell notifications, and block out FOCUS time in your calendar so others will not disturb you. Worried about missing something on e-mail? Set an auto-reply telling folks that you're not available for a set amount of time, or that you're in an important meeting—which you are: a meeting with yourself.

Maybe self-care is your focus and the first step is getting a pedicure. You'll still want to eliminate distractions, even when resting—to be fully present to experience the simple act of putting your needs first.

*"Follow **ONE** Course Until Successful."*

—Robert Kiyosaki

SCHEDULE IT

For most people, consistency is key to success. Typically, you'll see greater end results by dedicating small chunks of time daily to moving forward. But occasionally I meet people who get excellent results by "bingeing"—tackling their desired outcomes in bigger, longer, less frequent gulps.

What's important is to decide what's doable and then to schedule it in your calendar!

When I was working in corporate America, I had the dream of publishing an article for Corporate Communication International of New York. I was working during the day, so the only time to dedicate to my dream was in the evenings when I was back home. I set aside an hour every night for researching, writing, and rewriting.

Often I'd get so into it I'd continue into the wee hours, writing away. The result? That paper won a prize at the institute's annual conference and launched my career in corporate responsibility for a Fortune 500 company. See the power of applying focused, scheduled time to a specific destination?

"If it's not scheduled, it's not real."

—*Marie Forleo*

MAKE ONE MORE MAP
(YOUR <u>M</u>ONTHLY <u>A</u>CTION <u>P</u>LAN)

A simple six- or twelve-month action plan can help remind you where you're going and the steps you need to take to get there.

You can create your MAP electronically or on a sheet of paper or a piece of cardboard. I chose cardboard this year and wrote only my main vision elements. I then used an online calendar to drill down to specific daily and weekly actions—dedicated playtime with my daughter, for example.

What action steps can you spread across the next six or twelve months?

Download my twelve-month MAP template at **www.cortneymcdermott.com** or draw your own based on the following example. Then write down your focus areas for each month to keep you moving toward your destination.

Identify the exact steps you want to take for each, and schedule them into every month for the next six to twelve months.

"The secret of getting ahead is getting started. The secret of getting started is breaking your complex overwhelming tasks into small manageable tasks, and then starting on the first one."

—Mark Twain

Monthly Action Plan

www.cortinc.com

Instructions: Fill each Focus and Intention box with a short, clear Timbuktu (your next life or business destination).

	January	February	March
Q1 Focus			
Intention			

	April	May	June
Q2 Focus			
Intention			

	July	August	September
Q3 Focus			
Intention			

	October	November	December
Q4 Focus			
Intention			

DON'T MAKE EVERY PIT STOP

Even if you have your MAP and your schedule, if your time is interrupted by texts every five minutes or e-mail chimes every two, you can bet it'll take a good while for you to get where you're going.

It'd be like making every pit stop on your way from New York to California.

An essential part of focusing is eliminating *all* distractions during the time you've set aside to show up for your dreams. This is critical. I can't tell you how many well-intentioned people I've seen fail or delay the realization of their dreams only because they were continually distracted.

When I tell people that I habitually turn data off on my phone while I'm focusing on a project, they think I'm crazy. I'm convinced, on the other hand, that it's one of the smartest things I can do. The other option is simply not sustainable.

With your mobile data off, you can still receive calls. And since people rarely call nowadays, that means very few interruptions, but you're still keeping yourself available for family and anything urgent.

What you won't receive are constant e-mail/Instagram/Facebook/LinkedIn/Pinterest/WhatsApp, etc. interruptions. It's almost impossible to avoid the lure of those pings . . . so you have to protect yourself and your time.

You decide when to turn that setting back on, when to let your attention wander, instead of letting those distractions decide for you.

PS: THE SAME GOES FOR IN-PERSON INTERRUPTIONS! SO CLOSE THE DOOR, PUT UP A SIGN—ANYTHING TO (POLITELY) MAKE YOUR BOUNDARIES CLEAR.

TAKE A TIME-OUT

How can we stay focused on what's most important to us in a world that's so full of cheap and easy distraction?

We have to take TIME-OUTS . . . and the drastic measure of OPTING OUT.

In a society that admonishes us to "Go! Go! Go!" and to stay "on top of" current events and "up to speed" in our fields, a lot of what I'm suggesting may seem counterintuitive or feel uncomfortable to start.

But if you stick with it, you'll free up massive amounts of energy, and create a much more sustainable life while you're at it.

Here's a simple method I love, one that gets me through my most challenging days:

> *Drop everything you're doing. Take a*
> *time-out. Whatever you need—a moment,*
> *an hour, a day—just be with yourself. Yep,*
> *that's right: do absolutely nothing.*

I know how hard it is to do nothing. But it's also the first step out of the vortex of distraction and a *never enough* mentality.

You'll hear about some other ways to take time-outs later, so for now let's move on to my next secret: opting out.

IT'S OKAY TO OPT OUT

The easiest way to decide what to opt out of is by asking, "Does this platform/newsletter/[insert potential distraction here] inspire, educate, or entertain me?" and/or "Does it have anything to do with my Timbuktu?"

A few months ago, I opted out of all but three newsletter subscriptions. I chose to stay on those three because every update from these sources provides an opportunity to learn and grow and is also directly related to what's most important to me.

I also opted out of a couple social media platforms for the same reason. Business experts warned me, "You've gained a following and your clients are active on these channels." But my intuition was quietly countering, "Get off." So I got off.

All that noise wasn't inspiring me; it was draining me. The choice to remove myself freed up so much mental and creative energy and allowed me to be more present where it truly counts, like with my family.

What are three things you can opt out of *right now*?

A NOTE ABOUT YOUR INBOX

"E-mail is a great organizing mechanism
for other people's priorities."

—*Brendon Burchard*

E-mail is a phenomenal work tool. It instantaneously con-
nects us with people clear across the world and allows us
to move ideas faster than ever before.

There's an inherent overload in this kind of system,
though.

You know what I'm talking about if you've ever opened
your inbox in the morning, only to emerge hours later
wondering, *What just happened? Where did my morning
go?*

If that sounds at all familiar, these simple steps can help you regain control of your inbox and stay focused and purposeful while you're there.

1. **Schedule it.** Set aside specific times for e-mail and stick to them, and avoid starting or ending your day in your inbox. (Start and end with *your* priorities instead!)

2. **Read selectively.** When you open your inbox, scan for those e-mails that are most important to you and address them first.

3. **Don't skip around.** Read and respond to one e-mail at a time. If you know you can't respond right away, file that e-mail away as needing a response and set a date and time in your calendar when you can action it. By filing it away rather than continually going back to it, you're freeing up loads of mental space.

4. When your scheduled time for e-mail is up, **get outta there!** You can always come back to it in the next chunk of time you've set aside for e-mail, but now *you* are in control.

TUNE OUT TO TUNE IN

All the exercises from this chapter are designed to help you enter and stay in the gap, meaning you are closer than ever to where you want to be.

Because your long-term sustainability requires *tuning out* from the distractions and noise of others' priorities so you can *tune back in* in a way that serves you and creates the greatest ease in getting where you're going next.

PS: TUNING OUT FOR ME IS OFTEN AS SIMPLE AS TAKING A QUICK WALK AROUND THE BLOCK TO CLEAR MY HEAD. GIVE IT A WHIRL. IT WORKS!

Confidently Follow YOUR Intuition

WHAT ELSE CAN YOU RELEASE?

As you move through the process of getting rid of distractions, you might also find that you're holding on to
baggage that doesn't even belong to you. And it's weighing you down on your journey.

I once had a dream that I was on a bus and about to
reach my stop. As I stood up to get off, a bunch of my
dad's personal belongings fell out of my bag. I had to
decide whether to stay and pick them up and put them
back in my bag, or get off and leave them behind.

I decided to leave them behind and get off at my stop.

In my dream I felt so liberated . . .

What stuff are you holding on to that doesn't even belong to you? Can you let any of it go so you can arrive at your next destination faster?

LIGHTEN YOUR LOAD

*"You will find that it is necessary to let
things go; simply for the reason that they
are heavy. So let them go, let go of them. I
tie no weights to my ankles."*

—C. JoyBell C.

There's a scene in Cheryl Strayed's book *Wild* when a
new friend on the Pacific Crest Trail offers to help her
lighten her load, and she has to dump everything out of
her overstuffed backpack to figure out what goes back in.

It's great if someone with more experience or wisdom can help us in this process, but what if it's just us? After we've dumped out the contents of our bag, how can we determine what needs to go back in and what's just weighing us down?

The first key is to take it *one* bag at a time. If we go dumping out the contents of all the various areas of our life, we'll bury ourselves.

The second key is to take a moment with each piece and ask, does this light me up? If the answer is yes, it stays in the bag. If the answer is no, it's time to leave it behind.

Exercise

HOW TO LET GO OF EXTRA BAGGAGE

Here's a simple test for understanding what we need to let go of:

FEELS GOOD = STICK WITH IT

DOESN'T FEEL GOOD = RE-ADJUST OR LEAVE BEHIND

Here's how it works. Say, for example, in your relationship bag, you find that you complain a lot. Maybe you picked up this habit from your mother. It doesn't matter as much where it comes from as what you want to do about it.

Say every time you complain you have that icky "doesn't feel so great" feeling. Now you know that this is unnecessary baggage.

The next step is finding practices that feed the behaviors you want and starve the ones you don't.

So, for example, you could wear a tie bracelet on one wrist that you have to untie and then tie around the other wrist every time you complain. This mildly annoying inconvenience will start you on the track of starving the habit.

Also find a practice that reinforces what you do want: at the end of every day, you can rate yourself on a scale of 1 to 10 in terms of how you showed up in your relationship (1 = eek! / 10 = total rock star) and aim for as many 10s as you can. This tiny practice becomes a game that you want to win (and ultimately feeds the fire of a loving relationship).

LET YOUR FEELINGS LEAD

"Follow your bliss."

—*Joseph Campbell*

As you continue to lighten your load on your way to Timbuktu, remember to check in with yourself. You might get a gut reaction when something doesn't feel right. Or maybe for you it doesn't come from the gut. I've had clients describe it in many ways: a sinking feeling, a constricting can't-breathe-fully kind of sensation . . . Whatever it is, it's something inside that says *no*.

Have you ever noticed those times you went ahead with it anyway, whatever "it" was, and how the signals grew stronger and stronger and maybe you just kept ignoring them, until you got sick, or the deal fell through, or something else went awry? I know I have.

The opposite is true for when you're feeling really called to something—when you're not sure why but it just "feels right." Again this is your brain sending feel-good chemicals to your body, messages to go for it, and it's so important to follow that lead.

How simple things would be if we could just learn to listen and respond to those visceral reactions.

THE FUZZY FEELING MEANS YOU'RE CLOSE

Did you ever play that warm/sizzling, cold/freezing game as a kid? The one where the closer you got to what you were seeking, the warmer/hotter your playmate would announce you were?

That's still a great way to know if you're on the right track.

A cold, stomach-dropping sensation means hightail it out of there. You're looking in the wrong spot! Whereas your inner guide will often announce proximity to a soul goal with that warm, fuzzy (or bright-hot) feeling.

A new friend of mine recently decided to take what she's calling her "leap-of-faith tour." She left behind a life and choices that were making her unhappy to follow her lifelong dream of being a dancer. She's choosing to follow that fuzzy, bubbling, warm energy . . . and loving every minute of it.

PS: IS THERE AN ACTIVITY THAT ALWAYS GIVES YOU THAT WARM, FUZZY FEELING? FOR ME, IT'S READING, ESPECIALLY IN A BATHTUB! PAY SPECIAL ATTENTION TO WHATEVER IT IS FOR YOU, SINCE IT CAN HELP YOU TO RESET WHENEVER YOU NEED.

SHE WHO STOPS IS LOST

After passing the finish line of my first marathon in Venice, I went straight to my husband and collapsed into his open arms. "You don't know how many times I wanted to quit, to give up," I said. His soft reply was, "But you didn't, you didn't."

Joy flooded my body in that moment as those words rooted in: no matter how dark it got, no matter how impossible the endeavor seemed when I was in the thick of it, success came down simply to putting one foot in front of another to get me past that line.

There's a saying in Italian, *Chi si ferma è perduto.* "One who stops is lost." It takes courage and a special kind of grit to keep going, and you can have others supporting, encouraging, and reminding you of your ability to get where you're going. But in the end it's *your* race.

At times it'll feel euphoric, at others grueling, like you really can't take even one . . . more . . . step. But somehow you will. And that next step doesn't need to be a leap; it can be the tiniest forward motion in the direction of your vision.

Because the good news is that we get to decide what those steps look like. So many of the steps in a marathon actually feel good and full of purpose. So many don't. Trust your heart and see if you can remember that sometimes suffering holds the greatest gifts—like in childbirth, for example—and that it's the journey that enlivens us.

Plug Into Your PEOPLE

BUILDING YOUR DREAM TEAM

As you make your way, you're going to want people around you who can help you stay connected to your values and intentions. And if they've already been where you're headed, that's even better.

We are heavily influenced by the people around us. Human behavior expert Jim Rohn popularized the idea when he said, "We are the average of the five people we spend the most time with," and so we need to pay very careful attention to who's in our circle.

Don't worry. I'm not suggesting you abandon all your friends for newer, brighter versions.

Here's what I *am* proposing: start giving the majority of your time to people who inspire the daylights out of you.

As you seek out inspiring people to bring into your life, remember that study about "six degrees of separation"—the idea that we are only six connections away from anyone else.

And in today's hyperconnected world, that's probably more like two or three degrees. Which makes things much easier.

If you're looking to authentically connect with someone who's just a couple of degrees away, go for it. Ask for an introduction, connect on LinkedIn, send a fan letter.

Start building a team that builds you up.

Exercise

CLEAN UP YOUR RELATIONSHIPS

In order to build a healthy network, you need to understand whose energy helps you thrive and whose doesn't.

Ultimately, this exercise is about identifying the relationships you're valuing and why.

Step 1: Make a list of who is a **strength** in your inner circles, anyone who sparks joy and adds to your vitality (coworkers, friends, family members). Then add descriptions of people you need to bring into your immediate circles but whose name you do not know yet (for example, a new team member).

Step 2: Now make a separate list of **weaknesses** in your immediate circles. Who drains your energy and doesn't support your vision? Identify the people and groups (for example, a nagging friend or a frustrated associate), then add a description of the type of person/organization that could fit this list (for example, clients whose values aren't aligned with yours).

Now turn it into a **flow chart** with connections coming in and out of your immediate circles.

Your Circles of Influence

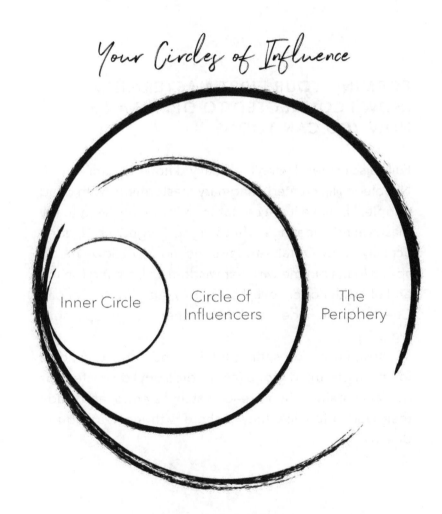

Inner Circle

Circle of Influencers

The Periphery

FORMING YOUR FIRST MASTERMIND (HOW I CONNECTED TO OPRAH AND HOW YOU CAN TOO)

Full disclosure: I don't actually know Oprah. But if Napoleon Hill created imaginary masterminds with dead people, I believe it's acceptable to invite the living to my mastermind meetings. That's right. Forget that I don't actually know Oprah—today's technology allows me to spend loads of time with her wisdom. I also hang (online and off) with Roger Love, Louise Hay, Alan Watts, Deepak Chopra, Marie Forleo, and many other straight-up inspiring peeps.

Now, I don't go setting a table and lighting candles for my mastermind group (as Hill did). But I do invite their guidance daily. When I read, watch, listen to, and study their work, I feel like they're there with me, leading me directly.

As the song goes, "Make new friends, but keep the old." You don't have to throw away any of your friends, just choose who you'll dedicate *most* of your time to. And remember, in today's world you can spend your time with anyone you want.

"Success leaves clues."

—*Anthony Robbins*

Find someone who's killing it in the area of your life and biz where you'd like to take it up a notch and *study them*. What are they doing differently? Study their psychology, their physiology, their spirituality.

Make it a point to learn something from them today—either by reading or listening to their work, or having a conversation with them if direct contact is possible.

PS: THE MORE YOU ABSORB THE TEACHINGS OF THOSE YOU ADMIRE, THE MORE YOU WILL MAKE THEM YOUR OWN, ADAPTING THEM TO YOUR OWN SPECIFIC NEEDS, DESIRES, AND STYLE.

IT TAKES A COMMUNITY

My sister sent me a hilarious coffee cup a few months ago. It read, *Behind every successful woman is herself.*

As funny as that is, it's also untrue.

The successful women (and men) I know surround themselves with people who share and help sustain their vision and values.

And from what I've seen, creating a supportive community online and off involves answering certain kinds of questions. For example:

> *How can I use what's important to me to serve and give back to others? How does my Timbuktu help other people connect with what they care about and with their vision for themselves?*

When you answer those kinds of questions—the ones that center around how you can serve—you have the keys to bringing together and positively influencing just about anyone.

Because here's the thing: plugging into your people isn't just about surrounding yourself with those who inspire and motivate you; it also means understanding how you can help others achieve what *they* want.

A SUSTAINABLE COMMUNITY

"To be interesting, be interested."

—*Dale Carnegie*

With your relationship flow chart in front of you, bring your attention to the arrows pointing inward. How can you move some of those people closer to your core? The best way I know to do this is by focusing on what those people want or need and considering how you might be able to help them get it.

The only resources you need to do this are time and creativity.

When I had very few resources, for example, I used my writing as a way to promote the work of those I most admired. I asked if I could interview them and share their message, promote their book, or advance their work in any other way. These leaders recognized my genuine enthusiasm and eagerness to give, and now I'm fortunate to consider a number of them friends.

Remember: we want to feed the fires that warm us and extinguish those that threaten to burn our house down. By keeping your attention on the arrows moving inward, you'll steadily be giving less import and energy to the ones on their way out. And that's the beginning of a sustainable community.

PS: YOU MIGHT WANT TO FOCUS ON ONE ARROW TO START. WHO COULD YOU REACH OUT TO TODAY?

PASS ON YOUR LIGHT

In a recent conversation with five-time *New York Times*-bestselling author Caroline Myss, we talked about how to share your truth in a noisy world.

Here's an excerpt from what Caroline said in that powerful interview:

> *"What is truth for me?" That's your first question. Spiritual inquiry is not about "Is there a God and does God answer my prayers? And can I get what I want?" That's a Santa Claus God. The question is "What is truth? And how do I act upon truth in my life with others?"*

> *What's the truth of my actions? What's the truth of my agenda with others? Why do I say what I say? What am I really*

up to here? Why can't I be honest with this person? Why am I addicted to this? Why don't I hold myself accountable for my emotions? Why am I passing on my suffering to a person who has nothing to do with it? Why am I punishing people because I'm not happy with my life?

That's what the spiritual path is. That's the spiritual life. Getting a grip on yourself. It's not hearing God and having visions. It's having the strength to get ahold of your darkness and not pass it on to others or pass it through yourself to others, instead to pass your light on to others.

How do you want to pass your light on to others? How do you want to share your truth, warts and all?

Transparency has two sides—what's going well and what's not. Good communication requires open celebration of victories *and* courageous admission of failures.

For example, one of the best pieces of sustainability reporting I've seen is by Engineers Without Borders. It's called the *Failure Report*, and it highlights all the struggles they had in reaching their Timbuktu of providing safe, clean drinking water to communities in need.

I'd like to see more organizations and people releasing failure reports. Because ultimately success is a by-product of failure. And it's not the fall but how you rise that defines you.

> *"There is no object so foul that intense light will not make beautiful."*
>
> —*Ralph Waldo Emerson*

CHOOSE A CHANNEL

To avoid the dimension of distraction we talked about earlier, it's best to choose one platform on which to begin sharing your story.

There are multiple ways to share our story online and off. Sometimes my favorite way to share is simply grabbing a cup of java with a friend at a local coffee shop; other times you'll find me onstage. The important thing is to do what feels good for *you*.

You might start by holding a local meet-up, writing a blog, pitching a piece for publication, or hosting a webinar. Or maybe you need to start simply sharing your truth in your daily life with those closest to you.

When and if you feel like it, you can move the conversation into social media as well.

PS: YOU CAN FIND ME ON INSTAGRAM BECAUSE I FEEL LIKE IT'S MORE ABOUT STORYTELLING THAN VOID SHOUTING. IT ALSO CREATES A DIGITAL PHOTO ALBUM TO REMIND ME OF THE DIFFERENT TIMBUKTUS IN MY LIFE.

Be Unforgettable.

Be Remarkable.

Be YOU.

"AT THE CENTER OF
YOUR BEING YOU HAVE
THE ANSWER; YOU
KNOW WHO YOU ARE
AND YOU KNOW WHAT
YOU WANT."

—LAO TZU

EACH CELL HAS ITS OWN JOB

Imagine we are all cells of the same body. For the body to function properly, we must each do our unique work. It is when we fail to do our own work that we create havoc in the body.

Picture a single cell looking over at another cell and thinking, *Ah, what he's doing looks interesting . . . Maybe I should give that a try,* or spotting a cell who's speeding along and thinking, *She's really got it made . . . I might as well just give up.*

It would be like an eye cell wanting to be a brain cell. Or deciding to just take the day off. *Yikes.*

When you think your contribution doesn't really matter and doesn't affect the whole, you're lost. When you ignore the impulses, or intuitive nudges, to move in a certain direction and look instead to others for answers, once again you are lost.

Each cell has its own job. And it must be carried out. How does one know what its job is? It just knows.

It is inherent. Built-in. With so many cells lost or not doing their work, how can the organism thrive?

One cell at a time.

BACK TO SIMPLE SUSTAINABILITY

One cell at a time means CHANGE STARTS WITHIN YOU.

This approach reinstates our power to make a difference, starting at the level of the self. It illustrates how when we are living and designing in accord with our deepest held values and desires, we really can reshape the world.

We don't need to be part of an assembly line.

Everything we've been talking about until now is about living by design rather than default, choosing long-term sustainability over the quick fix.

The following sections provide simple ways to continue the work you've done so far.

SUSTAINABLE LIVING PRACTICES: THE MIRACLE OF COMPOUND INTEREST

$$1 + 1 = 11$$

If I offered you $2.5 million today or one cent that would double in value every day for one month ($0.02 on day two, $0.04 on day three, and so on), which would you choose?

The best choice, as usual, lies somewhere in between.

Unless the month is February or you're Sir John Templeton, you'd be better off with the penny. At day 29 you'd have cleared the $2.5 million mark, by day 30 you'd have more than $5 million, and if it's January, March, May, July, or August, hello $10 million plus!

This is the miracle of compound interest.

Einstein found compound interest so powerful he deemed it the eighth wonder of the world. Because it doesn't just apply to numbers.

COMPOUND RESULTS OF GROWTH HABITS

The law of compound interest applies to *every* area of your life. It's why meditating for a few minutes a day is far more effective than one hour of meditation once a month. Or why writing out three things you're grateful for every night is more powerful than creating a one-page gratitude list at the end of the year.

The results may be hard to see at first (just like two cents, four cents, eight cents), but stick with it and you'll be absolutely blown away by your progress.

Bringing healthy growth habits into your life and applying them consistently leads to massive results. Any time you feel overwhelmed, your growth habits can help guide you back to living your purpose.

What's one growth habit you're committed to compounding through daily use? The pages that follow can give you some ideas.

NAP EVERY DAY

When my daughter used to take naps, she'd always list
the things she would do "tomorrow" (in other words, in
the afternoon). "Tomorrow I'm going to read *Duck for
President* and take Jackie Brown (her doll) for a walk and
make tea and cookies with candy hearts . . ."

   Naps are like that: they turn one day into two.

   Siesta is obligatory in my house, in my town, and
in Italy, where I live. Maybe it's just for twenty minutes.
Maybe you don't even fall asleep. But that time-out gives
you a whole fresh start.

It's now clear to me that "Go! Go! Go!" just doesn't hold up to scrutiny. We are *not* more productive when we spend ten hours a day in front of our computers with recurrent caffeine injections.

Still, sometimes I let my old-school mentality get the better of me: "You can't possibly take a nap today! There's way too much to do!" But on those days I find I accomplish much less and feel more stressed and less fulfilled.

BREATHE WITH YOUR BELLY

Now, I realize that taking a nap in the middle of the day is quite a luxury, especially for corporate employees, even if smarter employers are beginning to recognize its power. (Thank you, Arianna Huffington!)

Luckily, deep belly breathing works the same magic and is something anyone can integrate into office break time.

Here's the simplest way to get started: Inhaling through your nose, pretend there's a balloon in your belly and that you're filling that balloon with air. When the balloon is full, release your breath on a steady stream through your mouth. Repeat until you feel grounded and centered.

You can book ten minutes of private conference room time for this purpose, or set your phone alarm as a reminder to go outside for an inhale-exhale break every so often.

How are you breathing right now? Can you take some deep belly breaths? If that's too much, can you simply slow down your breath?

Deep breathing is the coolest and fastest built-in reset button we have. So if you want a sustainable life, use it regularly.

A NOTE ABOUT MEDITATION

Few of us can easily drop into a state of present-moment awareness by sitting still, closing our eyes, and breathing deeply. And that's okay.

Meditation doesn't have to be an hour-long seated practice. It's really any time we're fully engaged with the present moment. Maybe your meditation is drawing or writing or cleaning the dishes.

Give yourself permission to meditate this way throughout your day. You'll know you're doing it right because it will *feel good* and your breath will naturally flow with the activity.

SHAKE IT OUT

"You were once wild here. Don't let them tame you."

—Isadora Duncan

If you're in a funk, the easiest and fastest way out is through your body.

Thanks to Amy Cuddy, at Harvard, and other researchers in this field, we now know that jazzing up your body for even just two minutes actually configures your brain to be assertive, confident, and less stress reactive.

Give it a shot right now:

1. **Stand:** If you've been sitting for a while, go ahead and stand up and maybe even take this exercise outside.

2. **Stretch:** Take a full-body stretch. Breathe into any kinks or tight areas and see if you can begin to let go of any tension in those areas through the mindful use of your breath.

3. **Shake:** Starting with your feet and working your way up to your head, shake every part of your body. You might detect a lot of stiffness at the beginning (I was virtually unable to shake one of my legs when I first tried), but as you get better at it, this simple movement is so liberating.

If you followed along, you're feeling more body-mind energy than you did just a few minutes ago, and you're in a much better place to take on that next step on your life map.

I learned this shaking practice from Rochelle Schieck, founder of Qoya, a yoga-dance practice that has really helped me in my quest to remember who I am.

FOCUS ON THE GOOD STUFF

Here's a two-minute evening practice to set you up for success.

Right before hitting the pillow, write down three things you're grateful for from your day.

You'll want to choose a dedicated small notebook for this. If you're a notebook freak like me, go out and get a special one just for your gratitude journal. Keep the notebook right by your bed so you're sure to make this a habit.

The more you express genuine gratitude for the gifts in your life, the more those gifts will multiply.

This single simple act will also make you happier, healthier, and wealthier. Yes, wealthier.

Sir John Templeton, the multibillionaire who started with nothing, called gratitude "the secret to wealth."

So whatever it is—a smile from a stranger, knocking out your to-do list from that day, the walk you took with your dog—write it down!

PS: THERE'S A LOT OF SCIENCE BEHIND THE POWER OF GRATITUDE, SO IF YOU'RE ITCHING TO LEARN MORE, CHECK OUT SHAWN ACHOR'S HYS-TERICAL TEDX TALK *THE HAPPINESS ADVANTAGE*.

BABY STEPS TO THE ELEVATOR

"Never test the waters with both feet."

—Warren Buffett

The most important thing to remember as you play with these different sustainable living tools is to see what feels good for *you* and to put in that penny of practice every day.

Have you seen the scene in the movie *What About Bob?* when the obsessive-compulsive Bob, played by Bill Murray, discovers "baby steps"?

"Baby steps to the elevator . . . Baby steps onto the elevator . . ."

It doesn't take massive effort. If you've been sedentary and decide to prep for a 20k run, it might not be the wisest thing to head out for a 10k the very next day.

In other words, you don't have to leap and hope for the net. All that's needed is one steady step every day to live a sustainable life for *you*. It doesn't even need to be a large step; it can be a bit tentative and awkward, but you *do* have to take it.

KEEP THE CHANNEL OPEN

*"There is a vitality, a life force, a quickening
that is translated through you into action, and
because there is only one of you in all of time,
this expression is unique. And if you block it,
it will never exist through any other medium
and it will be lost. The world will not have it.
It is not your business to determine how good
it is nor how valuable nor how it compares
with other expressions. It is your business
to keep it yours clearly and directly, to keep
the channel open. You do not even have to
believe in yourself or your work. You have to
keep open and aware directly to the urges
that motivate you. Keep the channel open."*

—*Martha Graham*

The sustainable living steps we've covered together are part of an ongoing process of opening up to all the gifts that are inside you.

Remaining open and ready to receive is not always easy—I get that. But it's the most important work you can do, because it's the only way to raise your awareness and the collective consciousness of those around you.

And while none of us has a magic wand with which we can solve the world's problems, the mere act of showing up for these practices in your own life is enough to effect untold change.

EIGHT BILLION CELLS WAKING UP

"Lighthouses don't go running all over an island looking for boats to save; they just stand there shining."

—*Anne Lamott*

I believe that making a better world starts with *and within* you.

I believe that nurturing your needs and desires also nurtures the world.

I believe in the power of uncovering and living your own values, not someone else's.

I dream of eight billion cells waking up, radiating their truth out into the world, doing their unique work in service to the larger whole.

It's time: Be remarkable. Be unforgettable. Be *you*.

BECAUSE THAT'S THE ONLY WAY TO CHANGE THE WORLD.

Suggested Reading

- *Become What You Are* by Alan Watts
- *The Art of Possibility* by Rosamund Stone Zander and Benjamin Zander
- *Excuse Me, Your Life Is Waiting* by Lynn Grabhorn
- *The Happiness Advantage* by Shawn Achor
- *Three Magic Words* by Uell S. Andersen
- *The Artist's Way* by Julia Cameron
- *The Element* by Ken Robinson
- *Design the Life You Love* by Ayse Birsel
- *Thrive* by Arianna Huffington

Thank You

This book has many authors—all those who offered insights and smart criticism, who sat through the many versions of me that it took to give life to this dream, and whose support and gentle nudging shows on every page.

A hearty thanks to the team at Girl Friday Productions, notably Nicole Burns-Ascue for her impeccable guidance and seamless orchestrating, Laura Lee Mattingly for not leaving good enough alone, and Rachel Christenson for her design genius. Hilary Wilson: I am forever indebted to you for sparking this connection.

Many thanks also to my lucky stars: the names that line the praise pages—you are all an inspiration to me;

Amanda Pickens for your discerning eye and spirit; the Playfully Brave (Hil, Sal, Suze); Jo Yassumoto for being forever ready to wing it with me; Betsy Blankenbaker for knowing I could birth this baby long before I did; and Dave and Dana McDermott for always having my back.

Above all, I thank God for my husband Luca's unconditional support and love and for the miracle of our daughter, Gaia Ray . . . without you two there would be no Timbuktu.

About the Author

Cortney McDermott is an award-winning writer, speaker, and strategist to Fortune 500 executives, entrepreneurial leaders, and think tanks around the world.

Driven by her mission to inspire, educate, and activate the potential within each of us, Cortney redefines sustainability as the ability to sustain *yourself*. By looking within to make yourself a better person, you're making the world a better place.

Before turning entrepreneur, she served as an executive at Vanity Fair Corporation, vice president at Sustainability Partners, professor of graduate studies for several Big Ten universities, and global associate for the renowned beCause Global Consulting.

A graduate of the London School of Economics and a certified cultural mediator in multiple languages, Cortney also writes for a number of international publications, including *She Owns It* and the *Huffington Post*.

Cortney lives with her family in the United States and Italy.

CPSIA information can be obtained
at www.ICGtesting.com
Printed in the USA
LVHW01s0124090318
569212LV00002B/2/P